OXFORD REVISE

EDEXCEL GCSE

HISTORY

Early Elizabethan England, 1558–88

COMPLETE REVISION AND PRACTICE

Series Editor: Aaron Wilkes

Sarah Hartsmith

Tim Williams

Elena Stevens

OXFORD
UNIVERSITY PRESS

Contents

 Shade in each level of the circle as you feel more confident and ready for your exam.

How to use this book

This book uses a three-step approach to revision: **Knowledge**, **Retrieval**, and **Practice**. It is important that you do all three; they work together to make your revision effective.

 **Knowledge**

Knowledge comes first. Each chapter starts with a **Knowledge Organiser**. These are clear easy-to-understand, concise summaries of the content that you need to know for your exam. The information is organised to show how one idea flows into the next so you can learn how everything is tied together, rather than lots of disconnected facts.

Answers and Glossary

You can scan the QR code at any time to access sample answers, mark schemes for all the Exam-style Questions, a glossary containing definitions of the key terms, as well as further revision support go.oup.com/OR/GCSE/Ed/Hist/EarlyEliz

REVISION TIP

Revision tips offer you helpful advice and guidance to aid your revision and help you to understand key concepts and remember them.

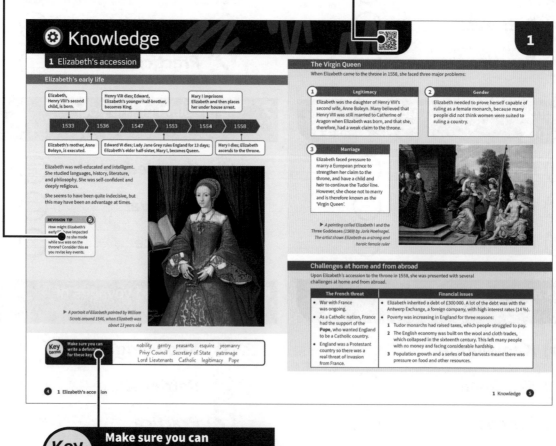

Key terms

Make sure you can write a definition for these key terms

The **Key terms** box highlights the key words and phrases that you need to know, remember, and be able to use confidently.

Retrieval

The **Retrieval questions** help you learn and quickly recall the information you've acquired. These are short questions and answers about the content in the Knowledge Organiser you have just reviewed. Cover up the answers with some paper and write down as many answers as you can from memory. Check back to the Knowledge Organiser for any you got wrong, then cover the answers and attempt all the questions again until you can answer *all* the questions correctly.

Make sure you revisit the Retrieval questions on different days to help them stick in your memory. You need to write down the answers each time, or say them out loud, otherwise it won't work.

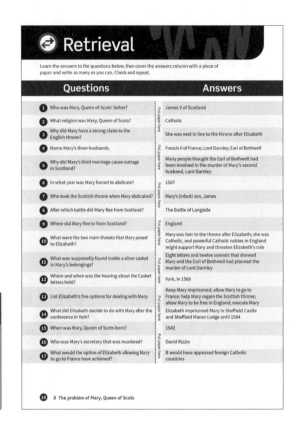

Previous questions

Each chapter also has some **Retrieval questions** from **previous chapters**. Answer these to see if you can remember the content from the earlier chapters. If you get the answers wrong, go back and do the Retrieval questions for the earlier chapters again.

Practice

Once you think you know the Knowledge Organiser and Retrieval answers really well, you can move on to the final stage: **Practice**.

Each chapter has **Exam-style Questions**, including some questions from previous chapters, to help you apply all the knowledge you have learnt and can retrieve.

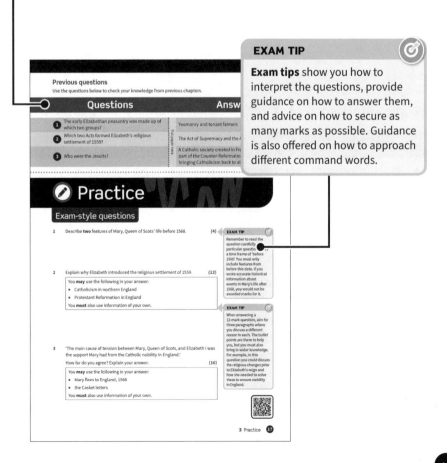

EXAM TIP

Exam tips show you how to interpret the questions, provide guidance on how to answer them, and advice on how to secure as many marks as possible. Guidance is also offered on how to approach different command words.

1 Elizabeth's accession

English society in 1558

Society in early Elizabethan times had a very rigid structure. The monarch was at the top, above all humans, with peasants towards the bottom, and non-living things right at the bottom. Everyone knew their place and few questioned it.

▶ *The structure of Elizabethan society was based on 'the Great Chain of Being'. It represented how Elizabethans ordered the world*

REVISION TIP

Think about how the structure of society in Elizabethan England underpins many of the key areas of content you examine in this time period.

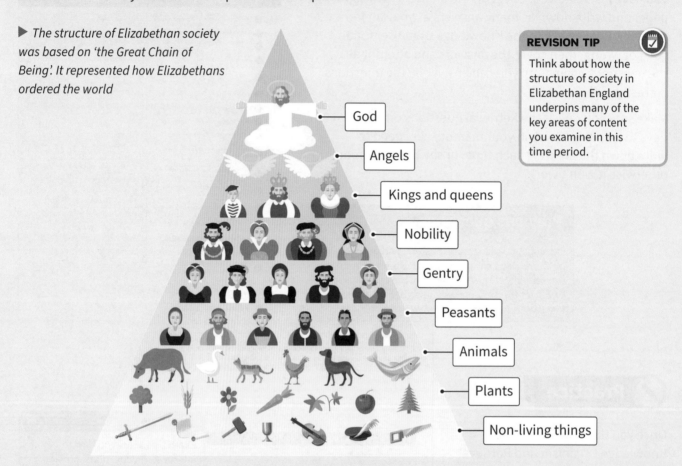

People were divided into three groups: the **nobility**, the **gentry**, and the **peasants**.

The nobility	The gentry	The peasants

• Most important members of society below the Queen.
 • Held titles like Duke or Lord, which were usually passed from father to son.
 • Owned large amounts of land, which provided income through rent.
 • Were the richest people in England, with an average annual income of £6000 per year (worth around £1 million today).
 • Could have a role in government.
	• The landlords of the countryside.
	 • Rented out land and were involved in business.
	 • Annual income of up to £200 per year.
	 • Might hold title of knight or **esquire**.
	 • Held positions of power, such as Justice of the Peace.
		• Poorest members of society.
		 • Made up of:
		   – **yeomanry**, who owned land or worked as servants to the nobility
		   – tenant farmers, who rented land.
		 • Worked the land and paid rent to their landlord.
		 • Life was challenging, often without enough food.

Government

The **Privy Council** was at the centre of the Elizabethan Royal Court. The Queen and the 19 influential men she appointed to the Privy Council could be described as the government of England at the time.

- The Privy Council was responsible for the day-to-day running of the country.

- Members of the Privy Council acted as Elizabeth's main advisers on important matters.

- Members of the Privy Council were chosen from the nobility, gentry, and Church, which meant that important Church figures could influence Elizabeth on governmental and policy matters.

- Elizabeth had to appoint the most powerful landowners to avoid possible rebellions.

- The **Secretary of State** led the Privy Council. William Cecil, Lord Burghley, held this role and was the Queen's most trusted adviser.

- The Privy Council did not have complete control over the governance of England. Elizabeth gave other key roles to people who were loyal to her. This was called **patronage**.

Patronage

Parliament

- House of Lords (nobility) and House of Commons (wealthy and educated gentry).
- Responsible for passing laws and involved in setting taxes.
- The Queen decided when to call Parliament and it was her choice whether she would listen to its advice.

Lord Lieutenants

- Appointed by the Queen to take responsibility for an area of the country.
- Settled disputes, raised taxes, and raised an army if asked to do so by the Queen.

Justices of the Peace

- Selected from the local gentry and appointed to keep law and order.
- Several per county, and around 1500 across England.
- Had to swear an oath to treat everyone equally.
- Could send someone to prison.

Life in early Elizabethan England

- Most people lived in towns or the countryside. A handful of cities, including London and Norwich, were growing.

- Most gentry and peasants depended on the wool, cloth, and wheat trades to survive.

  The wool and cloth trades were central to the English economy, but there had been a fall in demand after 1550.

- Religion was embedded into people's daily lives. All Christians went to church on a Sunday.

  Despite there being lots of religious change during the Tudor period, changes could be slow to reach local churches. Many people would have been confused and angry when their traditional **Catholic** practices were challenged.

- People of African descent were part of everyday life, working in a range of occupations across England.

⚙ Knowledge

1 Elizabeth's accession

Elizabeth's early life

| Elizabeth, Henry VIII's second child, is born. | Henry VIII dies; Edward, Elizabeth's younger half-brother, becomes King. | Mary I imprisons Elizabeth and then places her under house arrest. |

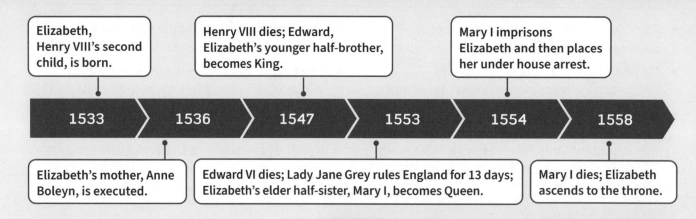

| 1533 | 1536 | 1547 | 1553 | 1554 | 1558 |

| Elizabeth's mother, Anne Boleyn, is executed. | Edward VI dies; Lady Jane Grey rules England for 13 days; Elizabeth's elder half-sister, Mary I, becomes Queen. | Mary I dies; Elizabeth ascends to the throne. |

Elizabeth was well-educated and intelligent. She studied languages, history, literature, and philosophy. She was self-confident and deeply religious.

She seems to have been quite indecisive, but this may have been an advantage at times.

> **REVISION TIP** ☑
>
> How might Elizabeth's early life have impacted the decisions she made while she was on the throne? Consider this as you revise key events.

▶ *A portrait of Elizabeth painted by William Scrots around 1546, when Elizabeth was about 13 years old*

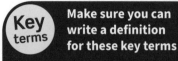 **Key terms** | **Make sure you can write a definition for these key terms**

nobility gentry peasants esquire yeomanry
Privy Council Secretary of State patronage
Lord Lieutenants Catholic legitimacy Pope

The Virgin Queen

When Elizabeth came to the throne in 1558, she faced three major problems:

1 **Legitimacy**

Elizabeth was the daughter of Henry VIII's second wife, Anne Boleyn. Many believed that Henry VIII was still married to Catherine of Aragon when Elizabeth was born, and that she, therefore, had a weak claim to the throne.

2 **Gender**

Elizabeth needed to prove herself capable of ruling as a female monarch, because many people did not think women were suited to ruling a country.

3 **Marriage**

Elizabeth faced pressure to marry a European prince to strengthen her claim to the throne, and have a child and heir to continue the Tudor line. However, she chose not to marry and is therefore known as the 'Virgin Queen'.

▶ *A painting called* Elizabeth I and the Three Goddesses *(1569) by Joris Hoefnagel. The artist shows Elizabeth as a strong and heroic female ruler*

Challenges at home and from abroad

Upon Elizabeth's accession to the throne in 1558, she was presented with several challenges at home and from abroad.

The French threat	Financial issues

• War with France was ongoing.
 	
• As a Catholic nation, France had the support of the **Pope**, who wanted England to be a Catholic country.
 	
• England was a Protestant country so there was a real threat of invasion from France.
	• Elizabeth inherited a debt of £300 000. A lot of the debt was with the Antwerp Exchange, a foreign company, with high interest rates (14 %).
	
	• Poverty was increasing in England for three reasons:
	
	  1 Tudor monarchs had raised taxes, which people struggled to pay.
	
	  2 The English economy was built on the wool and cloth trades, which collapsed in the sixteenth century. This left many people with no money and facing considerable hardship.
	
	  3 Population growth and a series of bad harvests meant there was pressure on food and other resources.

⇄ Retrieval

Learn the answers to the questions below, then cover the answers column with a piece of paper and write as many as you can. Check and repeat.

Questions | Answers

#	Question	Answer
1	What was the structure of Elizabethan society based on?	The Great Chain of Being
2	What two titles might gentry in early Elizabethan England have held?	Knight or esquire
3	The early Elizabethan peasantry was made up of which two groups?	Yeomanry and tenant farmers
4	What was the Privy Council?	The 'government' of Elizabethan England; the 19 men responsible for the day-to-day running of the country, who acted as Elizabeth's main advisers
5	What are the two houses in Parliament called?	House of Lords and House of Commons
6	What was the role of Justices of the Peace?	They were appointed to keep law and order in their county
7	In what year did Elizabeth become queen?	1558
8	Who was Elizabeth's mother?	Anne Boleyn
9	Why did people think that Elizabeth needed to get married?	To strengthen her claim to the throne by marrying a European prince, and to have a child and heir
10	Which country was England at war with at the start of Elizabeth's reign?	France
11	How much debt did Elizabeth inherit?	£300 000
12	Give one reason why poverty was increasing at the time Elizabeth came to the throne.	One from: Tudor monarchs had raised taxes / the English economy was built on the wool and cloth trades, which had collapsed / population growth and a series of bad harvests
13	Who were the most important members of society below the Queen?	The nobility
14	What were the three major personal problems Elizabeth faced when she came to the throne?	Legitimacy, gender, and marriage
15	Who was most of England's debt owed to?	The Antwerp Exchange
16	When did Mary I place Elizabeth under house arrest?	1554

Put paper here

 **Practice**

1

Exam-style questions

1 Describe **two** features of the nobility in Elizabethan England. **(4)**

2 Explain why Elizabeth did not have complete control over the way in which England was governed. **(12)**

> You **may** use the following in your answer:
> - Privy Council
> - Lord Lieutenants
>
> You **must** also use information of your own.

EXAM TIP

Before attempting to answer each question, use the 'BUG' method:

- **Box the command word**, so that you know what you are being asked to do.
- **Underline the key words** (the words that tell you which topic the question is about, and jog your memory about the topic).
- **Glance at the question again**, to pick up any additional information it is giving you and to help you picture what you need to do.

3 'Financial issues were the main problem that Elizabeth faced when she became queen in 1558.'

How far do you agree? Explain your answer. **(16)**

> You **may** use the following in your answer:
> - inherited debt
> - Elizabeth's legitimacy
>
> You **must** also use information of your own.

EXAM TIP

The bullet points are there to give you a way into the topic, but you will need to also discuss other problems Elizabeth faced when she came to the throne.

⚙ Knowledge

2 The religious settlement

The Church of England's role in society

- Religion was important in Elizabeth's Royal Court and she ensured her courtiers undertook religious worship.

- People's lives in England were organised around the religious calendar. Significant religious occasions were celebrated with feasts, festivals, and fairs.

- Everyone experienced the same religious ceremonies, such as baptism and marriage, no matter their position in society.

- Locally, the parish **clergy** were important figures in the community and encouraged people to live devout lives and helped them to understand Bible teachings.

Religious divisions in 1558

By 1558, there were deep religious divisions in England.

Henry VIII began the **Protestant Reformation** in England when he broke with Rome and the Catholic Church to divorce his first wife, Catherine of Aragon. In time, the Protestant Church of England was established in place of the Catholic Church.

Catholicism

- The main religion in England before the Protestant Reformation, with the Pope at its head.
- Catholics believe in seven **sacraments**, including baptism and marriage.
- Mary I (reigned 1553–58) reintroduced Catholicism after the reign of Protestant King Edward VI.
- In 1558, all religious services and most Bibles were in Latin.
- Catholicism was still widespread in the north of England some important noblemen still held Catholic services in their manor houses.

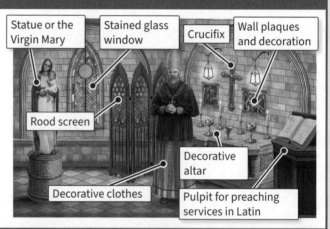

Statue or the Virgin Mary | Stained glass window | Crucifix | Wall plaques and decoration | Rood screen | Decorative altar | Decorative clothes | Pulpit for preaching services in Latin

Protestantism

- Named after Martin Luther and others who 'protested' against the problems they identified within the Catholic Church.
- Henry's son, Edward VI, consolidated the authority of the Protestant Church during his reign (1547–53).
- Protestants wanted the Bible to be in English.
- A radical group of Protestants, called **Puritans**, thought that the Reformation was not moving quickly enough.
- Many Protestants fled England during Mary I's reign, but began to return when Elizabeth was crowned.

- Puritans wanted to 'purify' the Church of any remaining Catholic influences to ensure people lived a simpler and more holy life.

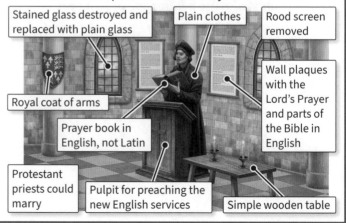

Stained glass destroyed and replaced with plain glass | Plain clothes | Rood screen removed | Royal coat of arms | Wall plaques with the Lord's Prayer and parts of the Bible in English | Prayer book in English, not Latin | Protestant priests could marry | Pulpit for preaching the new English services | Simple wooden table

The Elizabethan religious settlement

- Elizabeth's religious settlement was introduced in 1559 via two acts of Parliament: the Act of Supremacy and the Act of Uniformity.
- It attempted to heal religious divisions in England by creating a compromise that Elizabeth hoped would balance the demands of different religious groups and bring stability and peace.
- Protestantism was reinforced as the official religion in England, but some aspects of Catholic worship were allowed to remain.

1   The Act of Supremacy (1559)

- Elizabeth became Supreme Governor of the Church of England. This was controversial because the Pope did not have religious authority in England anymore.
- It was considered treason if someone in England did not acknowledge Elizabeth as Supreme Governor of the Church.
- All clergy members had to swear an oath of loyalty to Elizabeth.
- The Archbishops of Canterbury and York, as well as some bishops, stayed in their roles to help Elizabeth govern.

2   The Act of Uniformity (1559)

- Protestantism became the official religion in England.
- All churches used the English **Book of Common Prayer**, which included instructions on how to carry out religious services.
- The Book of Common Prayer and the Bible were printed in English.
- Everyone in England had to go to church weekly or they would be fined.
- Catholic Mass was abandoned.
- The wording of services was designed to appeal to both Protestants and Catholics, and churches were allowed to keep religious ornaments preferred by Catholics.

Impact of the settlement

- Most people in England supported Elizabeth's new religious settlement.
- The majority of the clergy swore the oath of loyalty.
- However, some Catholics were unhappy with the settlement's Protestant focus.
- A number of Puritans also objected to the settlement because some Catholic ideas and practices still featured.

> **REVISION TIP**
>
> When learning about the religious settlement, think about the causes, what the settlement contained, and its consequences. Why did Elizabeth need to introduce it? What were the key points of the acts? Who would be pleased and who would be annoyed by the settlement?

Knowledge

2 The religious settlement

The Catholic response to the religious settlement

- When Elizabeth came to the throne, Catholics worried she would want revenge for the persecution of Protestants under Mary I. Therefore, most Catholics welcomed the attempts at the peace and stability the religious settlement brought.

- Early in her reign, Elizabeth tolerated Catholics who were loyal and kept their faith private.

- Many of the most powerful and oldest noble families remained Catholic, including the Dukes of Westmorland and Northumberland, and many lived in the north of England. Elizabeth needed to keep these nobles on side so they did not pose a serious threat to her rule.

The papal bull

- On 27 April 1570, Pope Pius V issued a **papal bull** to his Catholic followers.

- This announcement **excommunicated** Elizabeth, officially excluding her from the Catholic Church, and called on all Catholics to remove her from power.

- English Catholics either had to do what the Pope wanted or remain loyal to Elizabeth. Every Catholic in the country was now a possible threat to Elizabeth.

Impact of the papal bull at home

- After 1570, the number of Catholic plots against Elizabeth increased.

- Elizabeth and her government became far less tolerant of Catholics.

- Laws were passed to limit the freedoms of Catholics in England; for example, it became treason to attend any kind of Catholic service.

Catholic threats from abroad

Threats to Elizabeth

Catholic powers in Europe

- Philip II of Spain proposed marriage to Elizabeth; Elizabeth rejected the proposal, angering Philip.

- France and Spain were both Catholic countries and two of the most powerful countries in Europe. They promised support for Catholic rebellions and plots against Elizabeth.

- France and Spain supported Catholic **missionaries** in England.

- Philip II of Spain attempted to invade England with the Spanish Armada in 1588.

Catholic missionaries

- The College of Douai, created in 1568 by English Catholic **cardinal** William Allen, trained missionary priests to travel to England to convert people back to Catholicism. The first of Allen's priests arrived in England in 1574. The college had the backing of the Pope and Philip II of Spain.

- The **Jesuits** were a Catholic society created in France in 1540 as part of the **Counter-Reformation**, which aimed to bring back Catholicism to all of Europe. One of the leaders of the Jesuit priests who came to England, Edmund Campion, was arrested and later brutally executed for encouraging rebellion.

Key terms — Make sure you can write a definition for these key terms

clergy   Protestant Reformation   sacraments   Puritans
Book of Common Prayer   papal bull   excommunicated
missionaries   cardinal   Jesuits   Counter-Reformation

Puritan grievances with the religious settlement

Most **Puritans** were unhappy with four key elements of Elizabeth's changes to the Church of England. They believed in the following principles:

1 Hierarchy

The Church should be run by ordinary people, no one should be head of the Church.

2 Decoration in churches

Church buildings should be undecorated (without stained glass windows, for example) so as not to distract from worshipping God.

3 Vestments

Clergy should wear plain clothes. The Act of Uniformity called for priests to wear a surplice, so Puritans were forced to comply, and it became known as the Vestment Controversy.

4 Church services

Church services should be solemn, without music and without the Catholic aspects of the Book of Common Prayer.

The extent of Puritan opposition

Even though they were unhappy, most Puritans did not pose a serious threat to Elizabeth.

- They were a minority in England.
- They had no powerful supporters in Europe.
- The fact that Elizabeth was not a Catholic was a sufficient reason to support her.

However, some did oppose her and Elizabeth took the possible threat seriously.

- Puritans organised prayer meetings in the 1570s that often included criticisms of Elizabeth's religious settlement. Edmund Grindal, the Archbishop of Canterbury, encouraged these meetings. Elizabeth viewed them as dangerous and, in 1577, she suspended Grindal and banned the meetings from taking place.

- In 1572, Puritan printing presses were destroyed after two pamphlets criticising the beliefs and structure of the Church of England were published.

- Elizabeth stopped MPs discussing all religious matters without her permission. When the Puritan MP Peter Wentworth challenged this, he was imprisoned.

Retrieval

Learn the answers to the questions below, then cover the answers column with a piece of paper and write as many as you can. Check and repeat.

	Questions		Answers
1	Which Church was established after Henry VIII's break with Rome?	*Put paper here*	The Church of England, which was Protestant
2	How many sacraments do Catholics believe in?		Seven
3	In which churches would you expect to see Bibles written in English?		Protestant churches
4	What did Puritans want to happen to help 'purify' the Church?	*Put paper here*	Puritans wanted to remove all remaining Catholic influences
5	Which two Acts formed Elizabeth's religious settlement of 1559?		The Act of Supremacy and the Act of Uniformity
6	What title did the Act of Supremacy give Elizabeth?		The Supreme Governor of the Church of England
7	What was the papal bull of 1570?	*Put paper here*	An official announcement from Pope Pius V, which excommunicated Elizabeth from the Catholic Church and called on all Catholics to remove her from power
8	Which two most powerful countries in Europe were also Catholic countries?		Spain and France
9	List three things that powerful Catholic countries did to support efforts to remove Elizabeth.	*Put paper here*	They promised support for Catholic rebellions and plots against Elizabeth; they supported Catholic missionaries in England; Philip II of Spain launched a full-scale attempt to invade England with the Spanish Armada in 1588
10	Who were the Jesuits?	*Put paper here*	A Catholic society created in France in 1540 as part of the Counter-Reformation, with the aim of bringing Catholicism back to all of Europe
11	List the four key elements of Elizabeth's changes to the Church of England that Puritans were unhappy with.		Hierarchy; decoration in churches; vestments; music and the Book of Prayer in church services

Previous questions

Use the questions below to check your knowledge from previous chapters.

Questions	Answers
1 What was the Privy Council?	The 'government' of Elizabethan England; the 19 men responsible for the day-to-day running of the country, who acted as Elizabeth's main advisers
2 Who was Elizabeth's mother?	Anne Boleyn
3 How much debt did Elizabeth inherit?	£300 000

Put paper here

✏ Practice

Exam-style questions

1 Describe **two** features of the Catholic response to the religious settlement. **(4)**

> **EXAM TIP**
>
> Read the question carefully to make sure you are clear on the specific topic you are being asked to describe, and stick to this in your answer. This question only asks you for two features, so you do not need to write any more than this.

2 Explain why Elizabeth had personal problems when she came to the throne in 1558. **(12)**

> You **may** use the following in your answer:
> - an heir to the throne
> - legitimacy
>
> You **must** also use information of your own.

> **EXAM TIP**
>
> In answering question 2, you need to write at least two separate paragraphs. You also need to go beyond the stimulus bullet points you are given with the examples you include in your response.

3 'Missionaries were the greatest Catholic threat from abroad to stability and peace in early Elizabethan England.'

How far do you agree? Explain your answer. **(16)**

> You **may** use the following in your answer:
> - College of Douai
> - papal bull of 1570
>
> You **must** also use information of your own.

Knowledge

3 The problem of Mary, Queen of Scots

Who was Mary, Queen of Scots?

- One of the most significant challenges Elizabeth faced came in 1568 when her cousin Mary, Queen of Scots, arrived in England.

- As the granddaughter of Margaret Tudor (Henry VIII's sister), Mary had a strong claim to the English throne: she was next in line after Elizabeth.

- Mary was Catholic, and a number of powerful foreign monarchs and influential English nobles wanted Mary to replace Elizabeth as Queen of England.

▲ A portrait of Mary, Queen of Scots, by François Clouet, painted around 1560–61

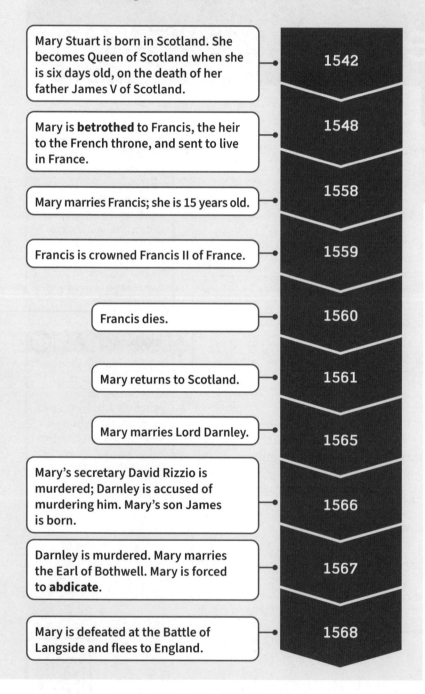

Mary Stuart is born in Scotland. She becomes Queen of Scotland when she is six days old, on the death of her father James V of Scotland.	**1542**
Mary is **betrothed** to Francis, the heir to the French throne, and sent to live in France.	**1548**
Mary marries Francis; she is 15 years old.	**1558**
Francis is crowned Francis II of France.	**1559**
Francis dies.	**1560**
Mary returns to Scotland.	**1561**
Mary marries Lord Darnley.	**1565**
Mary's secretary David Rizzio is murdered; Darnley is accused of murdering him. Mary's son James is born.	**1566**
Darnley is murdered. Mary marries the Earl of Bothwell. Mary is forced to **abdicate**.	**1567**
Mary is defeated at the Battle of Langside and flees to England.	**1568**

Mary comes to England

- Mary's marriage to the Earl of Bothwell was unpopular in Scotland, because Bothwell was widely believed to have been involved in the murder of her second husband, Lord Darnley.

- After Mary abdicated, the Scottish throne passed to her infant son James.

- Following her defeat at the Battle of Langside, Mary sought protection from her cousin, Elizabeth.

- Mary's Catholic faith put Elizabeth in a difficult position: powerful Catholic nobles in England might support Mary's claim to the English throne and try to overthrow Elizabeth.

The Casket letters

1. At a hearing in York in October 1568, eight letters and twelve **sonnets** that had been found in a silver casket containing Mary's belongings were presented as evidence against Mary.

2. The Scottish lords who opposed Mary's rule in Scotland claimed that these 'Casket letters' were written by Mary to the Earl of Bothwell in 1567 and showed that Mary and Bothwell had planned the murder of Lord Darnley.

3. The letters could be used to disgrace Mary, destroying her reputation so that she no longer posed a threat to Elizabeth. However, Elizabeth was reluctant to accuse Mary of murder.

▲ *The mysterious casket that supposedly contained letters and sonnets written by Mary to the Earl of Bothwell*

4. Darnley's death was investigated at a **conference** in York in 1569. Some believed that the letters were **forgeries** and had been planted in Mary's belongings. Despite this, people's suspicion of Mary increased and tensions between the cousins increased.

Elizabeth's options for dealing with Mary

Mary arrived in England in 1568 and was immediately taken to Carlisle Castle and treated as a prisoner.

Elizabeth had five options for how to deal with Mary:

1	Keep Mary imprisoned	This would stop Mary from contacting Catholic supporters.
2	Allow Mary to go to France	This would **appease** foreign Catholic countries.
3	Help Mary regain the Scottish throne	Mary would owe Elizabeth for her help, which might maintain peace between England and Scotland.
4	Allow Mary to be free in England	This would please the Catholic nobles and those who supported Mary at home and abroad.
5	Execute Mary	Eliminating Mary as a threat would send a powerful warning to potential Catholic rebels.

Mary was imprisoned in Sheffield Castle and Sheffield Manor Lodge between November 1570 and 1584.

> **REVISION TIP**
>
> Learn key evidence to support how Mary, Queen of Scots, was a threat to Elizabeth's position as Queen of England. Which are the key details that you could use in an answer?

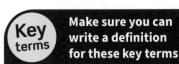

Key terms — Make sure you can write a definition for these key terms

betrothed   abdicate   sonnet   conference   forgery   appease

Retrieval

Learn the answers to the questions below, then cover the answers column with a piece of paper and write as many as you can. Check and repeat.

Questions	Answers
1 Who was Mary, Queen of Scots' father?	James V of Scotland
2 What religion was Mary, Queen of Scots?	Catholic
3 Why did Mary have a strong claim to the English throne?	She was next in line to the throne after Elizabeth
4 Name Mary's three husbands.	Francis II of France; Lord Darnley; Earl of Bothwell
5 Why did Mary's third marriage cause outrage in Scotland?	Many people thought the Earl of Bothwell had been involved in the murder of Mary's second husband, Lord Darnley
6 In what year was Mary forced to abdicate?	1567
7 Who took the Scottish throne when Mary abdicated?	Mary's (infant) son, James
8 After which battle did Mary flee from Scotland?	The Battle of Langside
9 Where did Mary flee to from Scotland?	England
10 What were the two main threats that Mary posed to Elizabeth?	Mary was heir to the throne after Elizabeth; she was Catholic, and powerful Catholic nobles in England might support Mary and threaten Elizabeth's rule
11 What was supposedly found inside a silver casket in Mary's belongings?	Eight letters and twelve sonnets that showed Mary and the Earl of Bothwell had planned the murder of Lord Darnley
12 Where and when was the hearing about the Casket letters held?	York, in 1568
13 List Elizabeth's five options for dealing with Mary.	Keep Mary imprisoned; allow Mary to go to France; help Mary regain the Scottish throne; allow Mary to be free in England; execute Mary
14 What did Elizabeth decide to do with Mary after the conference in York?	Elizabeth imprisoned Mary in Sheffield Castle and Sheffield Manor Lodge until 1584
15 When was Mary, Queen of Scots born?	1542
16 Who was Mary's secretary that was murdered?	David Rizzio
17 What would the option of Elizabeth allowing Mary to go to France have achieved?	It would have appeased foreign Catholic countries

Put paper here

Previous questions

Use the questions below to check your knowledge from previous chapters.

Questions		Answers
1	The early Elizabethan peasantry was made up of which two groups?	Yeomanry and tenant farmers
2	Which two Acts formed Elizabeth's religious settlement of 1559?	The Act of Supremacy and the Act of Uniformity
3	Who were the Jesuits?	A Catholic society created in France in 1540 as part of the Counter-Reformation, with the aim of bringing Catholicism back to all of Europe

Put paper here

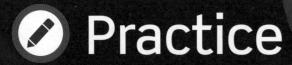 **Practice**

Exam-style questions

1   Describe **two** features of Mary, Queen of Scots' life before 1568.   **(4)**

> **EXAM TIP**
>
> Remember to read the question carefully. This particular question states a time frame of 'before 1568'. You must only include features from before this date. If you wrote accurate historical information about events in Mary's life after 1568, you would not be awarded marks for it.

2   Explain why Elizabeth introduced the religious settlement of 1559.   **(12)**

> You **may** use the following in your answer:
> - Catholicism in northern England
> - Protestant Reformation in England
>
> You **must** also use information of your own.

> **EXAM TIP**
>
> When answering a 12-mark question, aim for three paragraphs where you discuss a different reason in each. The bullet points are there to help you, but you must also bring in wider knowledge. For example, in this question you could discuss the religious changes prior to Elizabeth's reign and how she needed to solve these to ensure stability in England.

3   'The main cause of tension between Mary, Queen of Scots, and Elizabeth I was the support Mary had from the Catholic nobility in England.'

How far do you agree? Explain your answer.   **(16)**

> You **may** use the following in your answer:
> - Mary flees to England, 1568
> - the Casket letters
>
> You **must** also use information of your own.

⚙ Knowledge

4 Plots and revolts at home

The Revolt of the Northern Earls, 1569–70

In 1569, a group of powerful nobles from the north of England launched a rebellion against Elizabeth. This was one of the most significant challenges she faced during her reign.

REVISION TIP

For each of the plots and revolts against Elizabeth, what commonalities can you find? What specific key facts will you learn about each event?

Causes:

- After the religious settlement, Catholicism was still practised by many in private. In particular, the north of England remained largely Catholic; many Catholics there privately questioned Elizabeth's position as queen.
- Mary, Queen of Scots' arrival in England in 1568 meant some Catholics started to speak out about Mary being queen instead of Elizabeth.
- In 1569, Elizabeth refused to allow Mary to marry the Duke of Norfolk. He was a Protestant nobleman but came from a very powerful Catholic family. As a result, Norfolk left the Royal Court and headed north. He joined up with several northern nobles who were considering rebelling against Elizabeth.

Leaders:

- The Earl of Northumberland: a Catholic who had been treated well by Elizabeth.
- The Earl of Westmorland: a Catholic who had become powerful under Mary I and was married to a member of the highly influential Howard family.

Events:

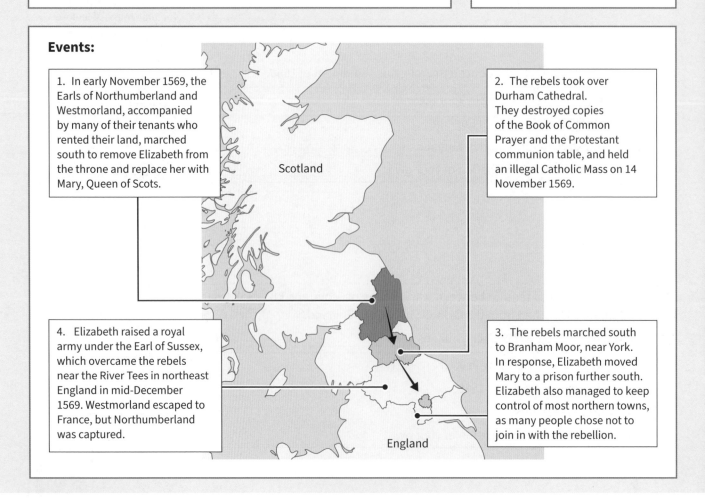

1. In early November 1569, the Earls of Northumberland and Westmorland, accompanied by many of their tenants who rented their land, marched south to remove Elizabeth from the throne and replace her with Mary, Queen of Scots.

2. The rebels took over Durham Cathedral. They destroyed copies of the Book of Common Prayer and the Protestant communion table, and held an illegal Catholic Mass on 14 November 1569.

Scotland

4. Elizabeth raised a royal army under the Earl of Sussex, which overcame the rebels near the River Tees in northeast England in mid-December 1569. Westmorland escaped to France, but Northumberland was captured.

3. The rebels marched south to Branham Moor, near York. In response, Elizabeth moved Mary to a prison further south. Elizabeth also managed to keep control of most northern towns, as many people chose not to join in with the rebellion.

England

Aims:

- ☑ Restore Catholicism as the official religion in England.
- ☑ Increase the power and influence of the northern nobles in England.
- ☑ Remove nobles who had guided Elizabeth's religious policies from power.

Outcomes:

- Northumberland was beheaded in York in 1572.
- Westmorland died in poverty in France in 1601.
- The Duke of Norfolk was imprisoned. (He was later released, only to get involved in another plot against the Queen.)
- Over 450 people were executed.

The failure of the Revolt of the Northern Earls showed the extent of support Elizabeth had across England. Elizabeth's opponents were frustrated they had failed.

Why did the Revolt of the Northern Earls fail?

Reasons for the failure of the revolt

Loyalty to Elizabeth	Lack of support from aboard	Lack of clear aims	Elizabeth responded effectively
Most Catholics remained loyal to Elizabeth, because they valued the tolerance and stability of her reign.	The rebels failed to get support from the Pope, France, and Spain, meaning the revolt did not have the strength it needed to succeed.	The rebels' aims were unclear: some focused on religion while others simply wanted to overthrow Elizabeth.	Elizabeth's response to the rebellion was well-organised and swift. Officials secured key towns in the north once the rebellion ended.

 Key terms Make sure you can write a definition for these key terms

cipher key   spymaster   treason   anointed   martyr

4 Plots and revolts at home

Plots against Elizabeth

After the papal bull of 1570, which called on all Catholics to remove her from power, Elizabeth faced several Catholic plots to overthrow her.

Causes	The plan	Failure and aftermath
1. The Ridolfi Plot, 1571		
Led by Roberto Ridolfi, an Italian banker who wanted to help English Catholics remove Elizabeth from power. After being released from prison for his involvement in the Revolt of the Northern Earls, the Duke of Norfolk lived under close guard. He became involved in the Ridolfi plot.	☑ Dutch Catholics, led by the Spanish Duke of Alva, would invade the south of England. ☑ English Catholics in the north of England would launch a second rebellion. ☑ Elizabeth would be murdered and replaced by Mary, Queen of Scots. ☑ Mary would then marry the Duke of Norfolk.	☒ Elizabeth's spies found coded messages and gold coins in the north of England. ☒ They cracked the code using a **cipher key** found under the doormat of Norfolk's house. ☒ Norfolk confessed his involvement and was executed in 1572. ☒ Ridolfi was abroad so he avoided arrest.
2. The Throckmorton Plot, 1583		
Developed by Sir Francis Throckmorton, who came from a powerful Catholic family. The plot was supported by the Duke of Guise, a French noble, and several Spanish nobles.	☑ The Duke of Guise would lead a French invasion, supported by Spanish troops. ☑ English Catholics would join the uprising to help secure Mary, Queen of Scots, as the new Catholic Queen of England. ☑ Elizabeth would be killed.	☒ Throckmorton was already under surveillance, so the plot was quickly discovered by Elizabeth's spies. ☒ Under torture, he confessed his involvement and was executed in 1584. ☒ Mary was placed under close guard, to ensure she was not involved in further plots.
3. The Babington Plot, 1586		
Anthony Babington planned to replace Elizabeth with Mary, Queen of Scots. He needed Mary's support for the plan.	☑ Babington and five other men would murder Elizabeth. ☑ Coded messages were sent to Mary, hidden in beer barrels that were taken to her room. ☑ Mary sent a reply, stating it was 'time to set the gentlemen [the assassins] to work'.	☒ One of Mary's servants worked for Elizabeth's **spymaster** and intercepted the letters. ☒ The letters were decoded using the cipher key, revealing the plot. ☒ Babington was arrested and executed in 1586. ☒ Mary was arrested, put on trial for **treason** and executed in 1587.

Why did the plots against Elizabeth fail?

Sir Francis Walsingham and the spy network: a large spy network existed across England that could uncover plots and respond to them quickly. As Secretary of State and spymaster, Walsingham was said to have 'eyes and ears' everywhere.

The lack of a popular alternative monarch: most English people, including Catholics, preferred an English queen to a foreign queen. Mary, Queen of Scots, was seen as untrustworthy because of her suspected involvement in her second husband's murder.

Why did the plots fail?

Elizabeth showed no mercy in punishing traitors: they generally faced torture and execution. The knowledge that any rebellion would be severely punished acted as a deterrent for would-be plotters.

The success of Elizabeth's religious settlement: it had been designed to keep most Protestants and Catholics happy, so only the most extreme groups of people opposed it.

Elizabeth's political skills: she was effective in dealing with Parliament and nobles. This meant few in power felt the need to rebel against her.

The execution of Mary, Queen of Scots

- The letter Mary sent to Babington gave Sir Francis Walsingham the evidence he needed to remove Mary as a threat. However, Mary denied that she had written the letter.

- Mary was found guilty of treason at her trial in October 1586. However, Mary was an **anointed** monarch, which made Elizabeth reluctant to sign the death warrant.

- The death warrant was signed on 1 February 1587, and Mary was executed on 8 February 1857.

▶ *This woodcut of Mary's execution would have been circulated to confirm that Mary had been killed and to discourage any future uprisings against Elizabeth*

The impact of Mary, Queen of Scots' execution

1 **Mary was viewed as a Catholic martyr**

Killing someone that had been placed in their role by God was seen as wrong. Many Catholics still thought Mary was important after her death, remembering her as a Catholic **martyr**.

2 **The threat from Catholic Spain intensified**

Mary's execution infuriated Philip II of Spain, because Mary was a Catholic queen. In response to Elizabeth's actions, he launched the Spanish Armada in 1588.

3 **Relations with James VI of Scotland remained positive**

James VI of Scotland, Mary's son, was the new heir to the English throne, but he was Protestant, so Catholics did not have a clear alternative to rally behind. James accepted Elizabeth's apology for Mary's death.

Learn the answers to the questions below, then cover the answers column with a piece of paper and write as many as you can. Check and repeat.

Questions

1	In what year did the Northern Earls launch a rebellion against Elizabeth?
2	Name the two rebel leaders of the Revolt of the Northern Earls.
3	What did the northern rebels do in Durham Cathedral in November 1569?
4	What did Elizabeth do to over 450 rebels in the aftermath of the revolt?
5	Give two reasons why the Revolt of the Northern Earls failed.
6	Why did the papal bull of 1570 increase the risk of a plot against Elizabeth's rule?
7	Give names and dates for the three main Catholic plots against Elizabeth after 1570.
8	Which plot included a plan for Dutch Catholics to invade the south of England?
9	Who were the key people behind the Throckmorton Plot of 1583?
10	How did the Throckmorton Plot plan to replace Elizabeth with Mary, Queen of Scots?
11	Who was Elizabeth's spymaster who helped uncover plots against her?
12	What role did a 'cipher key' play in the Babington plot?
13	What happened to Mary in 1586 after the Babington plot was discovered?
14	When was Mary, Queen of Scots, executed?
15	List two reasons why Catholic plots against Elizabeth after 1570 failed.

Put paper here

Answers

1569

The Earl of Westmorland and the Earl of Northumberland

Took over the cathedral; destroyed copies of the Book of Common Prayer and Protestant communion table; held an illegal Catholic Mass there on 14 November 1569

Had them executed

Two from: the majority of Catholics in England remained loyal to Elizabeth / lack of clear aims among rebels / no support from European Catholics / Elizabeth responded effectively to quash the rebellion

It was a clear order to all Catholics that it was their spiritual duty to oppose Elizabeth

Ridolfi Plot (1571); Throckmorton Plot (1583); Babington Plot (1586)

Ridolfi Plot

Sir Francis Throckmorton, the Duke of Guise, and several Spanish nobles

The Duke of Guise would lead a French invasion, supported by Spanish troops / English Catholics in England would join the uprising

Her Secretary of State, Sir Francis Walsingham

It provided the instructions needed to decipher the coded letters between Babington and Mary

She was arrested and put on trial for treason; she was found guilty in October 1586

8 February 1587

Two from: large spy network led by Walsingham uncovered plots / punishment of rebels discouraged potential plotters / no other popular alternative monarch / Elizabeth's religious settlement pleased most / Elizabeth was skilled politically, so few nobles rebelled

Previous questions

Use the questions below to check your knowledge from previous chapters.

Questions	Answers
1 What are the two houses in Parliament called?	House of Lords and House of Commons
2 Name Mary's three husbands.	Francis II of France; Lord Darnley; Earl of Bothwell
3 What were the two main threats that Mary posed to Elizabeth?	Mary was heir to the throne after Elizabeth; she was Catholic and powerful Catholic nobles in England might support Mary and threaten Elizabeth's rule

Put paper here

 Practice

Exam-style questions

1 Describe **two** features of the Throckmorton Plot (1583). **(4)**

> **EXAM TIP**
> There are 4 marks available for the 'describe' question. For each feature you need to develop your answer by adding extra detail about it. Aim to write four sentences in total.

2 Explain why Mary, Queen of Scots, was a threat to Elizabeth's rule. **(12)**

> You **may** use the following in your answer:
> - granddaughter of Margaret Tudor
> - Anthony Babington
>
> You **must** also use information of your own.

3 'Catholic plots against Elizabeth were unsuccessful due to the harsh punishments handed down to plotters.'

How far do you agree? Explain your answer. **(16)**

> You **may** use the following in your answer:
> - the religious settlement
> - Sir Francis Walsingham's spy network
>
> You **must** also use information of your own.

> **EXAM TIP**
> When writing your answer to the 16-mark question, spend between 25 and 30 minutes on it. There is also an additional 4 marks in this question for your spelling, punctuation, and grammar, and use of specialist terms.

⚙ Knowledge

5 Relations with Spain

Political, religious, and commercial rivalries

In the sixteenth century, England and Spain were two of the most powerful nations in Europe. They were rivals before Elizabeth came to the throne, and three key areas of conflict existed between the two: politics, religion, and **commerce**.

① Political rivalry

- Spain was the most powerful and wealthy country in sixteenth century Europe.
- English sailors like John Hawkins and Francis Drake attacked Spanish ships and ports and stole treasure. It was embarrassing and costly for Spain.
- Philip II of Spain had been married to Mary I, which had given him power in England. When Elizabeth became queen, Philip proposed to her but was rejected. Philip saw this as an insult.
- The Spanish had been partly involved in some of the Catholic plots to overthrow Elizabeth. Spain supported Catholic priests who were sent to England as missionaries to try and convert people back to Catholicism.
- Philip did not want England to build an alliance with France. This was a concern if Mary, Queen of Scots, became Queen of England, because she was a former Queen of France.

② Religious rivalry

- England was Protestant and Spain was Catholic.
- England had previously been Catholic under Mary Tudor and Philip II (1553–58), and before Henry's break from Rome (1534). Spain saw the Elizabethan religious **settlement** as an abandonment of the Catholic faith.
- The papal bull of 1570 made clear that Catholics should oppose Queen Elizabeth.
- The Spanish had been involved in the Ridolfi (1571) and Throckmorton (1583) plots, which aimed to replace Elizabeth with Mary as a Catholic queen.
- Spain also supported Catholic priests sent to England as missionaries.
- Tensions increased in the 1580s when Elizabeth's tolerance of Catholics declined, and any Catholic priest was automatically treated as a traitor.

③ Commercial rivalry

- From 1550, the wool trade declined.
- Spain already dominated 'New World' exploration, being in control of large parts of the Americas, including trade.
- England resorted to **piracy** to gain wealth from the Americas. They attacked Spanish ships and stole precious goods.
- Sir Francis Drake regularly engaged in piracy – although it was called **privateering**, as the Queen had given him permission to **plunder** on her behalf and share stolen good with the crown. In 1579, Drake captured the Spanish treasure ship *Cacafuego*, taking treasure worth around £30 million in today's money.
- English sailor John Hawkins started to capture, buy, and sell human beings, taking them from West Africa to the Americas. This was the beginning of England's involvement in the trade in enslaved Africans.

Drake's attack on Nombre de Dios, 1572: Drake attacked Spanish ships full of gold and silver anchored at the port of Nombre de Dios. He seized silver worth £20 000 (the equivalent of £4 million today).

English privateering

San Juan de Ulua, 1568: The Spanish attacked John Hawkins en route to the Americas. England seized control of a Spanish treasure ship heading to the Netherlands to pay Spanish soldiers.

The outbreak of war with Spain, 1585–88: English involvement in the Netherlands

England had a strong trading relationship with the Netherlands in the sixteenth century, mainly through the wool and cloth industries. Both countries had large Protestant populations.

Catholic Spain had ruled the Netherlands since 1556, which angered many Dutch Protestants.

In the early 1560s, Philip II had ordered Spanish troops in the Netherlands to enforce Catholicsm as the only accepted religion. He also introduced unpopular taxes.

This caused rebellion to break out across the Netherlands. Dutch prince, William of Orange, led a Protestant military campaign against Spanish rule.

Elizabeth responded to these events cautiously. Unofficially, England had backed the Dutch for a number of years, but Elizabeth was reluctant to support the rebellion militarily because that would lead to war with Spain.

Eventually, however, she agreed to support the Dutch Revolt, signing the Treaty of Nonsuch in 1585. This meant England was now at war with Spain.

Elizabeth sent her trusted adviser, Robert Dudley, to lead an English army in the Netherlands. However, Dudley did not get on with the Dutch and he returned to England in disgrace.

Spain kept control of the Netherlands.
Tensions between Spain and England continue to build.

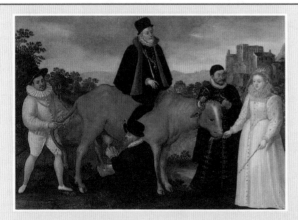

▲ This painting highlights the English and Spanish involvement in the Netherlands, which is represented as a cow. Philip II is riding the cow, while Elizabeth I and William of Orange stand by the cow's head. The Duke of Anjou, who had been in charge of the country on Spain's behalf, is pulling the cow's tail

The outbreak of war with Spain, 1585–88: Drake and the raids on Cadiz

- Francis Drake was one of England's most successful privateers.

- When war broke out between England and Spain in 1585, Philip II ordered a huge military **fleet** of ships to be assembled in the port of Cadiz in southern Spain. In 1587, Elizabeth ordered Drake to sail to Cadiz to attack the Spanish ships.

- When Drake's ships entered the Bay of Cadiz, a battle broke out. At least 27 Spanish ships were destroyed, and four ships were captured; the English took all the weapons and food onboard.

- The raid at Cadiz was a huge success for Drake and a huge embarrassment to Philip II. Drake referred to it as the 'singeing of the King of Spain's beard'.

- As a result, the Spanish had to delay their invasion plans for a year.

▲ A portrait of Francis Drake painted by an unknown artist around 1580

5 Relations with Spain

The Spanish invasion plans

Philip II of Spain planned to invade England and take the throne from Elizabeth. England would then be returned to the Catholic faith.

→

The Spanish fleet – the Armada – consisted of an impressive 151 ships, 7000 sailors, 34000 soldiers, and 180 priests and monks.

→

The fleet commander was the Duke of Medina-Sidonia, a well-respected Catholic noble. He was inexperienced in sea battles, but each ship was helmed by an experienced captain.

↓

Next, the Armada would sail to the English coast at Kent, and the soldiers would march to London. Most weaponry on board the ships was for this large land invasion.

←

The plan was that the Armada would leave Lisbon on 28 May 1588. It would then sail to Calais to collect soldiers from the Spanish Netherlands.

←

The fleet carried enough supplies to last four weeks, which was far more than the Spanish thought they would need.

↓

The Spanish Armada

In 1588, Philip II of Spain launched one of the largest naval fleets ever seen: the Spanish Armada.

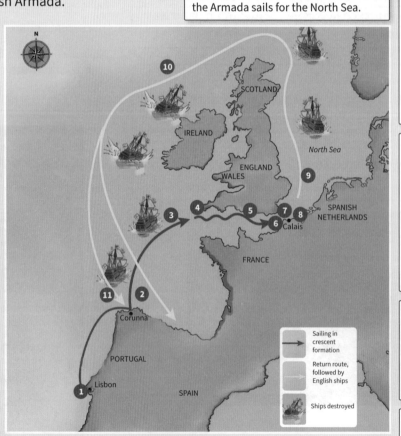

9 The Spanish route home through the English Channel is blocked, so the Armada sails for the North Sea.

8 8 August: At the Battle of Gravelines, the English inflict lots of damage on the Spanish. The Spanish ships cannot defend themselves in a sea battle. Medina-Sidonia tries to flee, but the English give chase.

10 Terrible storms off the coasts of Scotland and Ireland batter the Spanish ships. Many ships are wrecked. Survivors who make it to land are killed by the local population.

11 The Armada makes it back to Spain, suffering great losses: only 65 of the original 151 ships return. Philip is humiliated.

7 7 August: Drake leads an attack on the Armada using eight old English ships as **fireships**. These are sent into the Spanish fleet to cause chaos. To escape the flames, many Spanish ships cut their anchors.

6 6 August: The Armada arrives at Calais to pick up the soldiers from the Spanish Netherlands, but they are not there.

1 28 May: The Armada leaves Lisbon.

2 19 June: The fleet arrives at Corunna for final preparations.

3 21 June: The Armada sets sail for England in a crescent formation.

4 29 July: The fleet is spotted off the coast of Cornwall. The news is sent to London by lighting **beacons**.

5 31 July–4 August: The fleet is attacked by the English navy, but the Spanish suffer little damage.

Reasons why the Armada failed

English tactics	Spanish mistakes	The weather
☑ Commanders like Drake were skilled leaders and good tacticians. ☑ Using fireships broke up the strong Spanish crescent formation, making it easier for the English to attack the Spanish ships. ☑ The Spanish could not regroup at the Battle of Gravelines due to heavy bombardment by English cannons. ☑ The English ships were much faster than the Spanish ships.	☒ The famous Spanish warships were not designed for the rough English Channel and North Sea. They were larger, slower, and harder to manoeuvre than the English ships. ☒ The day's delay getting the soldiers on board at Calais gave the English more time to prepare. ☒ The Spanish underestimated the English navy. Their cannons were mostly designed for land battles, not sea battles. Also, their cannonballs did not fit the cannons on their ships. ☒ The commander, the Duke of Medina-Sidonia, was inexperienced.	☒ Most Spanish ships survived the battle, despite the Armada being defeated. It was violent storms in the North Sea on their journey home that meant more than half of the crew did not survive. ☒ The ships ran out of food and water as they struggled home in stormy weather. ☒ The surviving sailors were often unable to sail because of exhaustion and illness.

The aftermath of the Armada

Philip was humiliated but refused to accept defeat. He started planning a second Armada.

The victory united England, with most Catholics now putting their country before their faith. This helped to cement Protestantism in England.

Aftermath of the Armada

The defeat of the Armada was a pivotal moment for Elizabeth because it showed England was a major world power with a very powerful navy.

Elizabeth remained wary of the threat from Spain, France, or any other Catholic powers, so she continued to build up England's defences.

The English lost only 100 men compared to the Spanish who lost 20 000. However, thousands of English men later died of disease.

Key terms
Make sure you can write a definition for these key terms

commerce   settlement
New World   piracy
privateering   plunder
fleet   beacon   fireship

REVISION TIP

Learn the key points of what happened during the Armada and make sure you can describe them clearly.

Retrieval

Learn the answers to the questions below, then cover the answers column with a piece of paper and write as many as you can. Check and repeat.

Questions	Answers
1 Why had Philip II of Spain once held considerable power in England?	He had been married to Mary Tudor
2 Why was the piracy of Sir Francis Drake known as 'privateering'?	He had been given permission by Queen Elizabeth to attack foreign ships on her behalf, in order to steal their cargo and share the stolen goods with the crown
3 Which English sailor began England's involvement in the trade in enslaved Africans?	John Hawkins
4 Why was England on good terms with the Netherlands during Elizabeth's reign?	Both countries shared a strong trade in wool and cloth, and had large Protestant populations
5 Name the Dutch prince who led a Protestant military campaign against Spanish rule.	William of Orange
6 In which treaty did Elizabeth agree to provide support for the Dutch Revolt?	The Treaty of Nonsuch, 1585
7 Who did Elizabeth send to lead an army of English soldiers and cavalry in the Netherlands?	Robert Dudley
8 List the consequences of Drake's raid on Cadiz.	A battle broke out; at least 27 Spanish ships were destroyed; four ships were captured, and all weapons and food seized by the English; the Spanish had to delay their invasion plans for over a year; Philip II was humiliated
9 How did Drake refer to his success at Cadiz?	'Singeing of the King of Spain's beard'
10 Who commanded the Spanish Armada?	The Duke of Medina-Sidonia
11 From where did the Armada set sail on 28 May 1588?	Lisbon
12 Where was the Spanish Armada fleet anchored when Drake attacked using fireships?	Calais
13 Give two reasons why English tactics helped defeat the Armada.	Two from: skilled commanders like Drake were good tacticians / the fireships broke up the Spanish crescent formation, making it easier to attack / the English cannons constantly bombarded the Spanish at the Battle of Gravelines / the English ships were faster
14 How many of the 151 original Spanish ships made it back to Spain after the failed Armada?	65
15 Why was the defeat of the Armada a pivotal moment for Elizabeth's reign?	It showed England to be a major world power with a very powerful navy; it united England, with most Catholics now putting their country before their faith

Put paper here

Previous questions

Use the questions below to check your knowledge from previous chapters.

Questions	Answers
1 Why did Mary's third marriage cause outrage in Scotland?	Many people thought the Earl of Bothwell had been involved in the murder of Mary's second husband, Lord Darnley
2 Name the two rebel leaders of the Revolt of the Northern Earls.	The Earl of Westmorland and the Earl of Northumberland
3 Give names and dates for the three main Catholic plots against Elizabeth after 1570.	Ridolfi Plot (1571); Throckmorton Plot (1583); Babington Plot (1586)

Put paper here

Practice

Exam-style questions

1 Describe **two** features of England's involvement in the Netherlands during the early Elizabethan period. **(4)**

> **EXAM TIP**
>
> Make sure you are continuing to 'BUG' the question before you answer it. What is the command word in this question? What are the key words? Have you glanced back over the question to check before you start answering it?

2 Explain why the Spanish Armada failed. **(12)**

> You **may** use the following in your answer:
> - Sir Francis Drake
> - Spanish cannons
>
> You **must** also use information of your own.

> **EXAM TIP**
>
> A 12-mark 'explain' question should have three paragraphs that each give different reasons. The bullet points are there to help you, but you must include other information, too. For this question, you might also include how the Spanish warships were not suited to the conditions in the English Channel.

3 'The main reason why Catholic opposition to Elizabeth grew in the years 1558-88 was the papal bull (1570).'

How far do you agree? Explain your answer. **(16)**

> You **may** use the following in your answer:
> - Act of Supremacy and Act of Uniformity
> - Mary, Queen of Scots
>
> You **must** also use information of your own.

⚙ Knowledge

6 Education and leisure

How were people educated in early Elizabethan England?

- The **Renaissance** idea that society could be 'improved' through education grew during the early Elizabethan period.

- The increased use of printing presses in England meant it was much quicker and cheaper to produce books, so school teachers were able to use a wider variety of books in their teaching.

- Education was not compulsory, so people's education varied depending on their class and gender.

REVISION TIP

Aim to recall the differences in experiences of education in Elizabethan England, depending on gender, age, and class.

	Wealthy families	Lower-class families
Boys	• From the age of seven, boys went to **grammar school**. Entry was based on wealth, not ability. • The curriculum focused on Latin, English, and Religion. Younger boys were taught by older pupils until **'masters'** took over when boys reached the age of ten.	• Young boys went to **petty schools**, but only for a few years. Then they started work. • There was a focus on learning Bible teachings, as well as reading, writing, and arithmetic.
Girls	• Girls were taught at home by **private tutors**. Girls learned Latin and French, as well as dancing and music.	• Some girls went to **dame schools**, but only for a few years. Then they, too, started work. Dame schools taught a similar curriculum to petty schools.
Men	• From the age of 14, boys could study at **university**. Oxford and Cambridge existed in early Elizabethan England. • After university, men who hoped to become lawyers went to study at the '**Inns of Court**', where they would also live an exciting London lifestyle.	• Young men who could read and afford the fees could receive further education by joining a **guild**. Guilds were associations formed by different groups of craftsmen, such as carpenters, shoe-makers, and cabinet-makers. • Boys would be taken on as an **apprentice** at about the age of 14. In 1562, it became compulsory for anyone learning a craft through a guild to become an apprentice.
Women	• Education did not lead to a 'career' but provided women with the skills they needed to run a household or gain popularity at the Royal Court. • There were a few exceptions to this rule: for example, Mary Herbert, the daughter of a courtier, was a famous Elizabethan author.	• Women were not able to access further education in early Elizabethan England.

Key terms

Make sure you can write a definition for these key terms

Renaissance   grammar school   master   petty school
private tutor   dame school   university   Inns of Court   guild
apprentice   hawking   feast day   troupe   groundling

Leisure

- Elizabethans enjoyed a range of leisure activities and pastimes.
- What people did in their free time was generally based on their position in society. Activities enjoyed by the poor were usually free or cheap, while the rich used leisure activities as an opportunity to show off how fashionable and cultured they were.

Wealthy families	Both	Lower-class families
• The rich had access to vast parks to hunt for leisure. This included hunting deer on horseback or **hawking** (using a hawk to hunt smaller creatures). • Archery and fencing were popular. Men enjoyed tennis and bowls. • Musicians would perform in homes as entertainment, and guests would sing along. Some wealthy people, especially women, learned to play musical instruments. • Sewing and embroidery were popular pastimes for most women.	Theatres entertained all levels of society. From the backrooms and yards of inns and taverns to the great playhouses, theatre became one of the most popular leisure activities during Elizabeth's reign. 	• Inns and taverns were a place to drink and relax; they also provided entertainment, such as performances of plays. • People bet on the outcome of bloodsports, such as dog fighting, bear baiting, and cock fighting. • Cards and dice games were popular with men and women. • Wrestling, running, and Elizabethan football were very popular. • **Feast days** were especially popular because they meant a day off work. There was singing and maypole dancing.

Development of the early Elizabethan theatre

- When Elizabeth came to the throne in 1558, theatre barely existed in England.
- Plays performed by travelling acting groups (**troupes**) grew in popularity amongst the lower classes. The actors performed traditional stories in the backrooms of inns and taverns.
- Richer people began to take an interest in these plays, making financial contributions and turning the small troupes into acting companies.
- Eventually, the backrooms of inns and taverns were too small for the productions and the audiences. The Red Lion, the first purpose-built theatre, opened in London in 1567.
- In 1576, James Burbage opened The Theatre in Shoreditch, London. It was hugely successful and led to the opening of The Curtain in 1577 and The Rose in 1587.
- The nobility and gentry sat high up in galleries, while lower-class people stood in the pit, the area directly in front of the stage. They were known as 'groundlings' and paid a penny to enjoy a show.

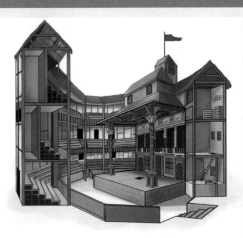

Retrieval

Learn the answers to the questions below, then cover the answers column with a piece of paper and write as many as you can. Check and repeat.

Questions

1 Name the period in Europe in which the belief grew that society could be 'improved' through education.

2 Why were schoolteachers able to use a wider variety of books in their teaching during the early Elizabethan period?

3 Why did most lower-class children receive no or little education during the early Elizabethan period?

4 Where did boys from wealthy families go to school from the age of seven?

5 Who taught younger boys in grammar schools?

6 Which schools taught boys and girls from poorer families?

7 What curriculum was taught in these schools?

8 Which two universities existed in early Elizabethan England?

9 What are guilds?

10 Which blood sports were enjoyed by lower-class people in early Elizabethan England?

11 Who were feast days especially popular with, and why?

12 Give three examples of entertainment and pastimes that were enjoyed by wealthy Elizabethans.

13 Which sports were popular with wealthy Elizabethan men?

14 Where were plays first performed at the start of Elizabeth's reign?

15 Name the first purpose-built theatre that opened in London, in 1567.

16 Who opened The Theatre in Shoreditch, London – and when?

17 What were the poor who stood in the 'pit' of a theatre known as?

Answers

The Renaissance

The increased use of printing presses in England meant it was much quicker and cheaper to produce books

Education was not compulsory; in many lower-class families, children had to be put to work at a young age

Grammar schools

Younger boys were taught by older pupils until 'masters' took over when boys reached the age of ten

Petty and dame schools

Bible teaching, reading, writing, and arithmetic

Oxford and Cambridge

Associations formed by people who worked in different skilled crafts, such as carpentry, shoe-making, and cabinet-making

Cock fighting, bear baiting, and dog fighting

The lower-class people of Elizabethan England, because it meant a day off work

Three from: sewing / embroidery / singing / music / hawking / hunting / archery / fencing / tennis / bowls / the theatre

Hunting, archery, fencing, tennis, and bowls

In the backrooms of inns and taverns

The Red Lion

James Burbage, in 1576

Groundlings

Put paper here

Previous questions

Use the questions below to check your knowledge from previous chapters.

Questions		Answers
1 Who was Elizabeth's spymaster who helped uncover plots against her?	Put paper here	Her Secretary of State, Sir Francis Walsingham
2 Why had Philip II of Spain once held considerable power in England?		He had been married to Mary Tudor
3 In which treaty did Elizabeth agree to provide support for the Dutch Revolt?		The Treaty of Nonsuch, 1585

 # Practice

Exam-style questions

1 Describe **two** features of the leisure activities of the wealthy in Elizabethan England. **(4)**

> **EXAM TIP**
>
> Read the question carefully; you must only describe leisure activities enjoyed by the rich. For example, one feature could be hunting. Theatre was enjoyed by all Elizabethans, so you could include this as an example, too.

2 Explain why England and Spain were rivals during the sixteenth century. **(12)**

> You **may** use the following in your answer:
> - commerce
> - religion
>
> You **must** also use information of your own.

> **EXAM TIP**
>
> Question 2 focuses on 'causes', so you need to explain why the event in question happened – in this case, the growing rivalries between England and Spain. Use causation language in your answer, such as 'This led to…', 'Consequently…', and 'Therefore…'

3 'Your experience of education in early Elizabethan England depended on your family's wealth and status in society.'

How far do you agree? Explain your answer. **(16)**

> You **may** use the following in your answer:
> - petty and dame schools
> - grammar schools
>
> You **must** also use information of your own.

⚙ Knowledge

7 The problem of the poor

Reasons for rising levels of poverty

- People without work were known as **paupers**, and they had to rely on charity to survive.

- The number of paupers increased during the early years of Elizabeth's reign. There were several reasons for this.

1 Rising population

England's population rose from 2.8 million to 4 million during Elizabeth's reign, as more people raised large families during a time of peace and stability.

2 Closure of the monasteries in 1530s

England's monasteries closed during the Protestant Reformation in England under Henry VIII. This meant the poor could no longer rely on monks and nuns to provide charity.

3 Enclosures

Farmers kept their sheep in enclosed areas ('**enclosures**') instead of letting them roam freely. This was more profitable for farmers, but meant fewer jobs and less land available for crops.

4 Increased taxes

Government taxation increased to pay for England's war against Spain.

5 Inflation

Across Europe, wages remained the same while living costs rose. This **inflation** meant the poor in society struggled to afford the basics they needed to survive.

6 Rack renting

Housing shortages meant some landlords massively increased rents on farmland. This process of '**rack renting**' meant many tenant farmers could no longer afford to live in rural areas and sought employment in towns.

7 Collapse of the cloth trade in 1550s

Many English people worked in the cloth trade, as weavers, spinners, and sheep farmers. The collapse left many people without jobs.

8 Poor harvests

A series of poor harvests, beginning the year before Elizabeth became queen and recurring in 1562, led to food shortages and higher prices for food.

Attitudes towards the poor

The idea of the '**deserving poor**' and the '**underserving poor**' shaped the way Elizabethans responded to the problem of poverty.

The 'deserving poor'	The 'undeserving poor'
<ul><li>People seen as not to blame for their poverty, including young, elderly, and disabled people.</li><li>Charities for the poor grew and **almshouses** were set up. Most wealthy people made occasional donations to charity.</li></ul>	<ul><li>People without a job who were seen as healthy and fit enough to work.</li><li>Known as the 'idle poor', many saw them as lazy, untrustworthy, and even criminal.</li><li>Seen by wealthy Elizabethans as a threat to the social order.</li></ul>

Vagabondage

In 1566, Thomas Harman published a book that explained the scams and tricks used by con artists known as '**vagabonds**' or 'untrustworthy beggars'. He accused some vagabonds of faking illness to get money by:

- cutting their skin to make themselves bleed, then deliberately infecting their wounds
- biting on soap to imitate frothing at the mouth and pretending to have a seizure
- pretending to have a mental illness by behaving in unusual ways.

Concerns over the rise in poverty

Puritan influence: Puritans in Parliament and on the Privy Council saw laziness as a sin and thought it was their duty to correct other people's behaviour.

Rebellion: People who lived in poverty might revolt against the Queen, as had happened before under previous monarchs.

Concerns over the rise in poverty in Elizabethan England

Social order: Travelling beggars challenged the established social order: they were not connected to a lord and did not follow any rules. People worried others might start to question the social order too.

Disease: Many believed that vagabonds and other travelling beggars spread diseases. There were plague outbreaks during Elizabeth's reign, in 1563, 1583, and 1586.

Crime: There was a rise in crime, and wealthy people were concerned about being robbed in the street.

Legislation dealing with the issue of poverty

	The Vagabonds Act, 1572	The Act for the Relief of the Poor, 1576
Deserving poor	<ul><li>Justices of the Peace kept a parish register of the deserving poor and paid for their food and shelter.</li><li>This was funded by the local poor rate, a special tax on the rich.</li></ul>	<ul><li>This law stated that some poor people were able bodied but genuinely could not find work.</li><li>Local authorities were responsible for finding work for the poor in their area.</li></ul>
Undeserving poor	<ul><li>Beggars over 14 years old were whipped and burned through the right ear.</li><li>A second begging offence would lead to imprisonment. A third begging offence could result in the death penalty.</li><li>Children of convicted beggars were forced to be servants for the wealthy.</li></ul>	<ul><li>Any paupers who refused to work when it was offered to them would be sent to a type of prison known as a '**house of correction**'.</li></ul>

 Key terms **Make sure you can write a definition for these key terms**

pauper   enclosure   inflation   rack renting   deserving poor
undeserving poor   almshouse   vagabond   house of correction

Retrieval

Learn the answers to the questions below, then cover the answers column with a piece of paper and write as many as you can. Check and repeat.

	Questions	Answers
1	What did the population of England rise to during Elizabeth's reign?	4 million people
2	What term was used to describe those without work in Elizabethan England?	Pauper
3	In which years of Elizabeth's reign were there poor harvests?	1562, 1565, 1573, 1586
4	What was 'rack renting'?	When landlords increased the rents on their farmland to extortionate levels that tenant farmers could not afford
5	What happened in the late 1550s that left many in the English cloth trade without a job?	The collapse of the cloth trade
6	How did England's war with Spain contribute to rising levels of poverty?	Government taxation increased
7	Who wrote a book in 1566 that explained the types of con artists and the tricks they were using?	Thomas Harman
8	What terms were used to describe these con artists?	'Vagabonds' and 'untrustworthy beggars'
9	How did some vagabonds supposedly fake illness to get money out of sympathy for medical treatments?	By cutting their skin to make themselves bleed, then infecting their wounds; by biting on soap so they foamed at the mouth and pretending to have a seizure; by pretending to have a mental illness by behaving in unusual ways
10	What two groups did Elizabethan society categorise the poor into?	The deserving poor and the undeserving poor
11	How did influential Puritans in Parliament and the Privy Council view the issue of poverty in England?	They saw laziness as a sin and thought it was their duty to correct other people's behaviour
12	Which Act stated that beggars over the age of 14 were to be whipped and burned through the right ear?	The Vagabonds Act, 1572
13	How did the classification of the poor change under the Act for the Relief of the Poor of 1576?	This stated that some poor people were able bodied but genuinely could not find work
14	What responsibilities were local authorities given under the Act for the Relief of the Poor of 1576?	Local authorities in towns and cities were responsible for finding work for the poor in their area
15	Under the Act for the Relief of the Poor of 1576, what happened to paupers who refused work when it was offered to them?	They were sent to a house of correction

Put paper here

Previous questions

Use the questions below to check your knowledge from previous chapters.

Questions	Answers
1 What were the two main threats that Mary posed to Elizabeth?	Mary was heir to the throne after Elizabeth; she was Catholic, and powerful Catholic nobles in England might support Mary and threaten Elizabeth's rule
2 Where did boys from wealthy families go to school from the age of seven?	Grammar schools
3 Give three examples of entertainment and pastimes that were enjoyed by wealthy Elizabethans.	Three from: sewing / embroidery / singing / music / hawking / hunting / archery / fencing / tennis / bowls / the theatre

Put paper here

Practice

Exam-style questions

1 Describe **two** features of education for girls in early Elizabethan England. **(4)**

2 Explain why Elizabeth's government was concerned about poverty in the early Elizabethan period. **(12)**

> You **may** use the following in your answer:
> - population increase
> - rebellion
>
> You **must** also use information of your own.

EXAM TIP

In answering this question, try to make links between the different reasons why Elizabeth's government was concerned. For example, you could explain how the rising population made food shortages due to poor harvests even worse.

3 'The attitude towards the poor in early Elizabethan England meant that the poor were always dealt with harshly.'

How far do you agree? Explain your answer. **(16)**

> You **may** use the following in your answer:
> - The Vagabonds Act (1572)
> - almshouses
>
> You **must** also use information of your own.

EXAM TIP

For the 'How far do you agree?' question, you need to weigh up evidence and come to a judgement in relation to the statement given. Decide to what extent (how much) you agree or disagree with the statement, and then support your view with specific knowledge.

⚙ Knowledge

8 Exploration and voyages of discovery

Causes of the 'age of exploration'

The 'age of exploration' (around 1400–1600) was a period when European countries like Spain, Portugal, and England were exploring the world and creating new routes across the sea. It was caused by several factors.

1   **Developments in shipping technology and navigation**

During the early part of Elizabeth's reign, important developments in shipping technology (see spider diagram below) meant ships could travel further and explorers could be more ambitious.

The **magnetic compass** helped navigation, as it always pointed North.

The **astrolabe** calculated the position of the sun and stars, helped determine a ship's location, and was used to work out the time.

The **printing press** meant maps could be mass-produced and standardised, and distributed more easily than hand-drawn maps.

Developments in shipping technology and navigation

Developments in **mapping techniques** in the fourteenth century spread from Italy, across Europe and into England. Flemish map-maker Gerardus Mercator created a map in 1569 that helped explorers use latitude and longitude more accurately.

Improved ship design: 'galleon' ships were large ships developed during the early Elizabethan period. They had many decks, so could hold lots of supplies. They were also reliable and stable in all weather conditions.

2   **Awareness of trading opportunities**

These developments expanded trade routes, opening up places for merchants to buy and sell goods, and providing new sources of wealth.

Explorers tried to find sea routes to wealthy nations like India and China, which were only accessible via long overland routes.

3   **Challenging Spanish dominance**

Spain's powerful navy had established an empire overseas, but Elizabeth was determined to beat the Spanish in empire-building and in trading.

By weakening Spain's power globally, Elizabeth's position on the English throne would be more secure.

> **REVISION TIP** ☑
>
> Consider the different causes. Which do you think was most important in enabling exploration to increase during Elizabeth's reign? Think about how you would explain why.

The impact of the expansion of trade

- New English-owned trading companies were formed. For example:
  - The East India Company traded tea and spices in India, China, and Japan.
  - The Levant Company traded wines and silks with Turkey and the Middle East.
  - The Muscovy Company traded timber and furs with Russia.
- Luxury items were highly valued in England and many traders made great profits as a result.

- In 1562, John Hawkins was one of the first English sailors to become involved in the transatlantic trade in enslaved Africans. He attacked Portuguese ships, and took enslaved Africans to the Caribbean, where they were sold to Spanish settlers.
- In the years that followed Hawkins' voyage, other people realised there were opportunities to make large amounts of money from the trade in enslaved Africans.

Drake's circumnavigation of the world

Francis Drake was the first English person, along with his crew, to circumnavigate the globe.

He set sail from Portsmouth on the south coast of England in December 1577, on his ship *Golden Hind*.

His main aim was to reduce the wealth and power of Spain by:

- ☑ attacking Spanish settlements on the west coast of South America as revenge for Spanish attacks on English ships
- ☑ taking Spanish treasure for himself and for his investors: many wealthy Elizabethans, including the Queen, helped pay for the expedition in the hope they would make money from the treasure brought back
- ☑ finding new lands to claim for England and Elizabeth
- ☑ finding new trade routes for England to access new wealth.

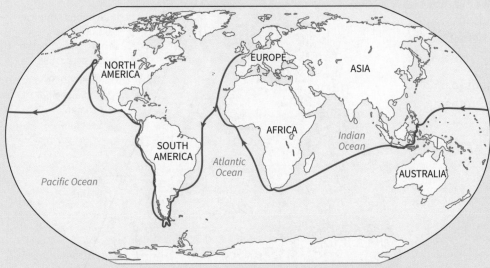

▲ *A map showing Drake's circumnavigation of the globe*

Why was Drake's voyage significant?

- Drake and his investors became wealthy. He brought back treasures worth roughly £200 million in today's money.
- Drake claimed new land for Elizabeth, including Nova Albion (New England). He also established new trade routes from the Indian Ocean.

- There was an increased understanding of how the world looked, which meant maps became more accurate.
- Tension between England and Spain increased because of Drake's actions. They were one cause of the Spanish Armada of 1588.

8 Exploration and voyages of discovery

Indigenous North America

- **Indigenous** Americans had inhabited every region of North America for centuries. There were hundreds of different Indigenous nations, with distinct languages, lifestyles, and customs.

- Indigenous American nations managed their land for the resources they needed. Across America, many Indigenous nations had developed sophisticated farming systems growing maize (corn) and other crops such as gourds (e.g., pumpkins). In the east, these farms supported towns.

- Like the Elizabethans who tried to colonise their land, Indigenous societies were hierarchical, with people with special skills and specialised roles considered most important. Leadership was carried out by chiefs who were advised by councils.

- The English were not the first colonisers of North America: Spain in particular had been successful in establishing colonies there and in South America for around 100 years before the English.

Colonising Virginia

In 1578, Elizabeth gave explorer Humphrey Gilbert official backing – a **patent** – to try to claim lands in North America on England's behalf.

When Gilbert was unsuccessful, Elizabeth transferred the patent to Walter Raleigh, Gilbert's half-brother.

Raleigh made two attempts to establish a colony in Virginia, on Roanoke Island.

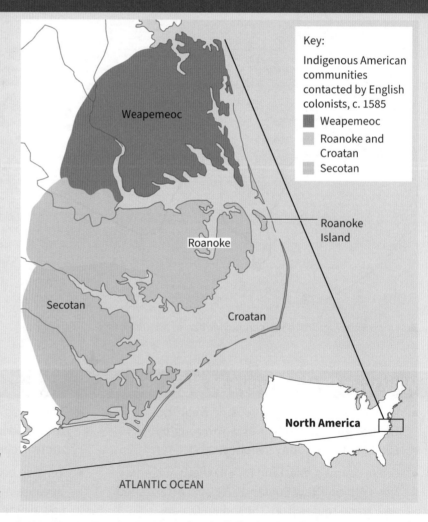

Key:

Indigenous American communities contacted by English colonists, c. 1585

- ■ Weapemeoc
- Roanoke and Croatan
- Secotan

Weapemeoc

Roanoke

Secotan

Croatan

Roanoke Island

North America

ATLANTIC OCEAN

▶ *The location of Roanoke Island and the Indigenous American communities contacted by English* **colonists**, *c.1585*

Key terms — Make sure you can write a definition for these key terms:

navigation   magnetic compass   astrolabe   circumnavigation
indigenous   patent   colonist

Roanoke Island: the first attempt at colonisation

| Sailors Philip Amadas and Arthur Barlowe set out to find a site that is suitable for an English colony on the east coast of North America. | Raleigh sends a fleet of 7 ships and 600 colonists from Plymouth to the area of Roanoke Island. | The English establish a colony on Roanoke Island. Ralph Lane is made governor.

Grenville leaves the island, intending to return to England to gather more colonists and supplies to bring back to Roanoke Island. | A fleet of Drake's ships offers to leave supplies for the Roanoke colonists but a ship is lost in a storm. Governor Lane decides to evacuate the Roanoke colony and return to England. |

April 1584 〉 **July 1584** 〉 **April 1585** 〉 **June 1585** 〉 **August 1585** 〉 **Nov/Dec 1585** 〉 **June 1586**

| Amadas and Barlowe meet with people from the local Croatan and Secotan communities. | One of the ships is damaged, and the fleet lands on Roanoke Island.

English Commander Richard Grenville orders colonists to explore local villages. An English silver cup is reported missing. Grenville accuses the people of Aquascogoc of theft, and burns down the village and its crops as punishment. | Relations with local people worsen. The English colonists' food begins to run out, and the Secotan tribe refuses to continue to supply them with food. |

Raleigh names the region on the east coast of America (including Roanoke Island) 'Virginia' in honour of Elizabeth.

Roanoke Island: the second attempt at colonisation

| Ships carrying 100 colonists, including women and children, arrive at Roanoke Island to establish a permanent settlement. They find the abandoned remains of the first attempt of the colony.

The new governor, John White, meets with Croatan people who explain the first colonists were killed by people from the Secotan, Aquascogoc, and Dasamonquepeuc communities. In revenge, White attacks the village of Dasamonquepeuc, despite the community showing no hostility towards English settlers. | White returns to Roanoke Island. When he arrives, there is no sign of the colonists. The only trace is a tree that had the letters 'CRO' carved into it. |

July 1587 〉 **August 1587** 〉 **November 1587** 〉 **August 1590**

| Relations between the colonists and Indigenous Americans deteriorate. The colonists decide to move the settlement to a different part of the island.

White leaves Roanoke to travel to England to bring back more supplies and colonists. | White arrives in England. Elizabeth bans all ships from leaving England in case they are needed to fight the Spanish. |

The missing settlers became known as the 'Lost Colonists'. Historians continue to debate what happened to them.

Retrieval

Learn the answers to the questions below, then cover the answers column with a piece of paper and write as many as you can. Check and repeat.

Questions	Answers
1 When and what was the 'age of exploration'?	A period around 1400–1600, during which European countries such as Spain, Portugal, and England explored the world and created new routes across the sea
2 Identify two developments in shipping technology and navigation during the Elizabethan period.	Two from: improved ship design / the magnetic compass / improved maps / the printing press / the astrolabe
3 Who created a map in 1569 that helped explorers use latitude and longitude more accurately?	Flemish map-maker Gerardus Mercator
4 What is John Hawkins remembered for?	He was one of the first English sailors to become involved in the transatlantic trade in enslaved Africans
5 Name the ship in which Francis Drake set sail from Portsmouth in 1577.	*Golden Hind*
6 What did Drake achieve in this ship?	He was the first English person to circumnavigate the globe
7 Which island on the east coast of North America did England want to colonise?	Roanoke Island
8 In what year did Walter Raleigh send seven ships from Plymouth to colonise the east coast of America?	1585
9 Which Indigenous American village did Richard Grenville blame for stealing a silver cup and consequently burn down in revenge?	Aquascogoc
10 When did Governor Lane decide to evacuate the first Roanoke colony and return to England?	June 1586
11 Why could John White not return to the colony after coming back to England to get more supplies in 1587?	Elizabeth stopped all ships leaving the country in case they were needed to fight the Spanish
12 When did White return to the colony and what did he find?	August 1590. He found no sign of the colonists. The only trace was a tree that had the letters 'CRO' carved into it

Put paper here

Previous questions
Use the questions below to check your knowledge from previous chapters.

Questions	Answers
1 Give names and dates for the three main Catholic plots against Elizabeth after 1570.	Ridolfi Plot (1571); Throckmorton Plot (1583); Babington Plot (1586)
2 What was 'rack renting'?	When landlords increased the rents on their farmland to extortionate levels that tenant farmers could not afford
3 Which Act stated that beggars over the age of 14 were to be whipped and burned through the right ear?	The Vagabonds Act, 1572

Put paper here

✎ Practice

Exam-style questions

1 Describe **two** features of the development in shipping technology and navigation during the early Elizabethan period. **(4)**

> **EXAM TIP**
> Remember to include specific facts in your answer. For each of the two features, you need to add an additional detail to get full marks. For example, if you stated that mapping techniques developed, you could then give the specific detail that Mercator's 1569 map helped explorers use latitude and longitude more accurately.

2 Explain why attempts by the English to establish a colony on Roanoke Island between 1584 and 1590 were unsuccessful. **(12)**

> You **may** use the following in your answer:
> - lack of food
> - attack on the village of Dasamonquepeuc
>
> You **must** also use information of your own.

3 'The most important reason for the rise in poverty in England in the years 1558–88 was the increase in population.'

How far do you agree? Explain your answer. **(16)**

> You **may** use the following in your answer:
> - enclosures
> - increased taxes
>
> You **must** also use information of your own.

> **EXAM TIP**
> As Question 3 contains the word 'important', this shows the key concept you are being asked to explain is significance. So, you need to compare how significant different reasons for the rise in poverty were during Elizabeth's reign.

Great Clarendon Street, Oxford, OX2 6DP, United Kingdom

Oxford University Press is a department of the University of Oxford. It furthers the University's objective of excellence in research, scholarship, and education by publishing worldwide. Oxford is a registered trade mark of Oxford University Press in the UK and in certain other countries.

Written by Sarah Hartsmith

Series Editor: Aaron Wilkes

The publisher would like to thank Elena Stevens and Tim Williams for their work on the first edition of Edexcel GCSE History (9-1): Early Elizabethan England 1558-88 Student Book (978-1382029759) on which this revision guide is based.

First published in 2023

British Library Cataloguing in Publication Data
Data available

978-1-382-04041-9

10 9 8 7 6 5 4 3 2 1

The manufacturing process conforms to the environmental regulations of the country of origin.

Printed in the UK by Bell and Bain Ltd, Glasgow

Acknowledgements
The publisher and authors would like to thank the following for permission to use photographs and other copyright material:

Photos: p4: GL Archive / Alamy Stock Photo; **p5:** ART Collection / Alamy Stock Photo; **p14:** Album / Alamy Stock Photo; **p15:** Marco Secchi / Alamy Stock Photo; **p21:** Pictorial Press Ltd / Alamy Stock Photo; **p25(l):** ART Collection / Alamy Stock Photo; **p25(r):** GRANGER - Historical Picture Archive / Alamy Stock Photo.

Artwork by Carlo Molinari, Rudolf Farkas, Moreno Chiachierra, Integra Software Services, Aptara Inc., and Newgen Publishing.

Every effort has been made to contact copyright holders of material reproduced in this book. Any omissions will be rectified in subsequent printings if notice is given to the publisher.

Although we have made every effort to trace and contact all copyright holders before publication this has not been possible in all cases. If notified, the publisher will rectify any errors or omissions at the earliest opportunity.

Links to third party websites are provided by Oxford in good faith and for information only. Oxford disclaims any responsibility for the materials contained in any third party website referenced in this work.